praise fo
Grief and Her Th

"Lovelady's nature-infused poems in *Grief and Her Three Sisters* are streaked with the silver gray of wisdom, pride and acceptance. And, as typical of a fine writer, his personal journey is transformed into one that so many of us recognize.

As he says in his poem, *Such is Poetry*, these are 'words to mend…troubled souls.'"

— Hiram Larew, *Mud Ajar*
(Atmosphere Press, 2021)

"Each poem has a life of its own, breathing with life, love and loss. Lovelady's work touches each reader with familiarity comparing his thoughts and emotions to our own self-reflections. We can all connect these threads with our own whether being in love or in loss. The subjects of each poem are insightful and deeply moving in breaths that breathe life into the readings. Beautifully discharged from his heart to his keystrokes, to each page we readers see even our own reflections upon the pages."

— Myrtle Thomas, *As Time Goes By: a Year Down the Road*
(Amazon self-published, 2021)

grief

and her

three

sisters

grief

and her

three

sisters

p o e m s

Jerry Lovelady

atmosphere press

Author's Note

<u>Grief and Her Three Sisters</u> is my third undertaking, following *Other Worlds, in Other Words* and *The Wasted Space Between Your Ears*, the latter being an E-book published in 2019, available only on Amazon-Kindle. This is not a collection of love poems so much as it is a collection of poems about those hopelessly driven by love and the various aspects living life with and without love can bring. Many of the more gut wrenching situations described here are real and written from my own experience.

Malice is not a factor in any of my poetry. My writings routinely disdain social injustice, poverty and racism. Some of the poems in this book admirably reflect this bias on my part. Since they are such good targets, I enjoy deriding the perpetrators of ethnocentrism. Since I am not a journalist, I am free to choose sides and write about whomever I feel needs discussing or cussing, not necessarily in that order.

In a world that seems quite short of love right now I hope that this book eases some of the heartaches. We can never share 'enough humor, spread enough joy, make enough fun or confront overarching power with hard won truths, no matter what the consequences may be. All are spontaneous acts of love in their own right, behaviors which I believe should be put into practice wherever and whenever possible.

"When your tail is dragging, hold your head up.
You make your own luck, son."

May Landry—(Spring of 1974)

Table *of* Contents

Part Three: A Rhapsody for Contrite Hearts

Part Four: Simple Songs of Meager Self-Awareness

Part One

The

River

Gods

"When we speak of Nature we are actually speaking of the process which transfigures and transcends this existence we recognize into something else."

From "The Great River Taketh", 2021

The Great River Taketh

This season the river took away several inches
of topsoil before it retreated back behind its high banks.
That flood uncovered a large patch of wild onion plants.
No way to tell how many years they had lain dormant there.
In May their pale, white florets gave them away.
That and an odor only an onion makes when it is cut.

I mowed around them till they had bloomed out
so they might multiply in the rich loam, pre-planted
at the just the right depth for growing onions.

In death there is always life.
In a seed there is hope for life.
In our offspring resides all genetic diversity.

Nature conquers in numbers uncountable,
the scale of which boggles the mind.
Each mowing strikes down millions.
Millions more spring up to replace the fallen.
Each specimen is repeated, perfect in its creation.

None mourn their lack of identity.
In subjugating ranks they usurp my peaceful yard,
the neighborhood, the township, the county,
the state, the territory, the whole continent, with
only the ocean and providence to stop their progress.

Even then their seeds are scattered on restless tides,
washed up on foreign soils to propagate, undeterred.
Unyielding, these foreigners are barely kept at bay
for a while, for the span of our short lifetimes.

One must admire their tenacity as they devour
any abandoned house or un-kept, manmade structure.
Their certain restlessness is played out in run down
neighborhoods as weeds, vines and rains slowly
reclaim the boards, the roofs, even the foundations,
till all is an almost unrecognizable, massive
festering of competing organisms.

No way to call a truce, man looks on helplessly.
However tragic or beautiful, it is the way of all
things to pass from their former shapes and existences
into something else unfamiliar, or unrecognizable.

When we speak of Nature we are actually speaking of
the process which transfigures and transcends this
existence we recognize into something else.

So, I am not frightened when I hear someone talking
to the trees,
making their best bargain with that which transforms
and transcends,
already knowing that they will not be cheated.

In the Pale Dawn Hours

In the creeping hours before sunrise
        tired eyes stare at nothingness.
The wind soughs sad and breathless
        to a heartless cold Moon.
She coyly hides her light behind
        the grey silhouetted cloud banks.
Precluded and forbidden are
        her salving silver rays.
The seeds of a faithless lover's promise
        were callously planted here yesterday.
Like alien mushrooms they sprouted and invasively
        expanded in the darkness.
Love is a private party invitation
        addressed to the sufferers,
        attended only by its victims.
Strangers never dream
        of fully feeling
        Love's depth of desolation.
Caverns might be carelessly bored through
        deadened hollow hearts and go unnoticed.
New encounters are met with high piled stones
        which block all the exits.

In the morning after a speared Sol
        bleeds speckled gold and yellow droplets.
Healing cumuli and nimbi medics will
        quickly perform CPR.
Knots will be tied, the sunrise hurriedly
        knitted back together again.
Splendid silver sutures of light
        will be pulled through the satin skin

of a lacerated Dawn.
A dramatic daybreak bleeder will erupt
in a bloody patchwork sky.

Blind gods will sign to us
in the cryptic vernacular
of an unknown tongue.
They will pose ridiculous riddles
about Love and other enigmatic events,
unable to witness our reactions.
Uncaring and oblivious to it all,
we shall grudgingly rise from our beds
to forge on through another blissless day
without a clue.

Headstones Set in Rows

Though not completely straight,
they stand with rigid spines and
swerve between the shell topped
road and its oak tree sentries.
This is the road which brings the dead
to their final destination.
This is where I come to find you
on days I need to remember.

About a year has passed.
Greedy weeds have barely
had time to take root.
January's rains have pummeled
the Christmas flowers sister Jan left,
now limp and moldering
in the early morning sun.
Bright green and red ribbons wave
tattered and tired of the shredding winds.
From east to west the sun faithfully
warms your well-kept graves
with silent resolution.

No shade tree for your interment site
laid beside Momma under a wide open sky.
No shadows to intrude on your peace.
Her name, birth and death dates were
carefully incised in pink granite relief,
chiseled inside the outline of Louisiana,
the state where she was born.
You share a headstone made for two,

your information also carved, inside the outline
of Texas, your birthplace.

We honored your collective wishes to be forever
united on this shared stone memorial.

My mind's eye sees your rugged face
etched in scratchy lines, like the barbed wire
fences we erected on your homestead
long ago in another, better time and place.
I remember that aged wonder of a face posed,
rifling through the Sunday newspaper.
A determined face that beamed at the task
of erecting the miles of barbed wire
we pulled in the hot sun and stapled onto
black creosoted fence posts we planted.

In straight lines those posts marched
up and down the wooded hills,
through small rills and mud holes,
through briars and brambles.
We chopped trails through crowded thickets
with cane knifes and double-bit axes.
No chain saws for us, no gloves either.
Just grit and determination on our faces,
sweat and skinned knuckles,
sunburned necks and shoulders.

Bologna sandwiches with cheese was our lunch,
with a cold soft drink at the end
of the long day and all the water

you could stand to drink.
You paid me one silver dollar a day
for all my toils.

I did not know we were poor then.
We were rich with the land--
land poor, to be exact.
You did not see us that way, though.
We were creating a legacy, you said.
A short lived legacy that you
liked to claim was your destiny, but
which never completely came to fruition.

None of us could rescue that destiny
for you, so you finally gave up trying.
Then, we gave up trying.
Now, here we are, you in the grave,
me just this side of it
breathing in and out,
trying to remember.

I picture your tanned face and dark hair
under a construction worker's hard hat
pulling miles of electrical wire through conduits.
Incalculable lengths were accumulated over four decades of
pulling that wire and connecting it to circuitry
for the various industries you helped to build.
All that so you could buy us shoes,
cars and college educations.

You required no thanks.
We gave back so little.
You gave so much more than that to me.

My memory of you parts the grief and gives me some solace.
Even though I get little thanks for what I do,
you have taught me that it is enough
just to receive the thanks
I give to myself for the choices I have made.

Rain on a Tin Roof

Rain at night sings the most
pleasant songs, lulls my aching,
crowded brain to sleep.

Rain at dawn clouds my windows with
thick fog, adds an edginess
to my thoughts.

The usually sharp corners of my mind
become uselessly rounded off.
I wield a blunt object defending myself from boredom.

Scattered clues get strewn around like breadcrumbs
to entice me; clues which I pathetically follow.
Laughing birds devour them after I pass.

Deeper, ever deeper into
the forest of doubt and anxiety I heedlessly stroll,
never expecting to be waylaid or lost.

Suddenly, like a shadowy mugger, out jumps boredom.
Give me all your time, patience and ambition,
it sinisterly demands and I wordlessly comply.

Maybe I am wrong for giving in so easily.
The grass needs mowing, the weeds are getting taller.
Why does it have to rain on my most optimistic days?

God must put something in the rain that encourages general
slothfulness, some sort of sublime lethargy.
My bed does not care if I doze away the whole day.
Beds are good like that.

The rain is pounding holes in that tin roof.
The tall grass and healthy weeds loudly applaud.

Our Cabin in the Woods

Our place stood strong against a flood
that Spring when all the neighbors fled.
Packed four feet deep in sticks and mud,
yet we reclaimed our old homestead.

The vandals wrecked our quiet home
in the dark forest near a stream.
A peaceful place of solitude;
our place to rest, to share our dream.

Through broken panes thieves crawled inside,
took little we had hoped to use.
Caused quite a mess of things we loved.
Our small treasures showed some abuse.

We cleaned things up and patched the panes,
the broken shards swept from the floor.
We mended screens against the bugs,
repaired the damaged, kicked in door.

For simple want of our desires,
we owned the place to get away.
No price too great, no cost too high
we deemed unfit or balked to pay.

The years have tasked us with a chore;
restore our cabin's former grace
so we might come to play once more.
Pray the River lets us keep our space.

Mowing as Dharma (1)

After morning coffee I don my old straw hat,
prepared to attack the transgressing weeds.
The mower growls into action and I am already
thinking about sitting down and meditating
over a cold glass of tea.

Munching and rending, mulching and pulverizing;
that is the mower's mantra.
Its dirty deed is done with merciless efficiency.
The work winds round a circuitous path cut
between the tall wild persimmon trees and water oaks.

Here and there sprout the scattered progeny of other trees.
Huckleberry, sweetgum, yaupon and mimosas spring up,
unprompted and unwanted.
They are the youthful hopes of far too many different
species vying for the same space in my shady yard.

I like the persimmons best.
They feed the wildlife each Autumn with their sweet,
succulent fruit containing either a spoon, knife
or fork shaped seed hidden inside their sugary flesh.
I always avoid their pale green shoots and tender
stems when I mow.
Just starting out in life, they do upasana to their gods.
I, Shiva of the yard, show them mercy.

Long ago I made a pact with the tall persimmons.
If they promised not to fall on my house,
I promised that I would not mow down their offspring.
So far, the persimmons have kept up their end and

I have kept mine, with only a few mishaps.
So, the yard is dotted with small trees,
most of which will never live more than a season,
their Karma already sealed forever.

I Have No Children to Brag About

Nothing ever came of my earnest efforts.
If I did, I would love them deeply and faithfully.
The fertile years for starting a family
have ignored me altogether.

The trees and rivers have become my children.
As fortune would have it, I adopted them,
or maybe they adopted me.
Perhaps it was a mutual arrangement.

I write long letters about them
to a preoccupied world.
I write about the grasses and trees.
How tall they have gotten.
I express how much my children's
steadfastness, constancy and devotion
pleases me.

They will outlive me by centuries.
My undistinguished passing
will bring them no grief.
Their inheritance will be a treasury of words.
Words so deftly written they will
turn grown men's hearts to mush.

Perhaps I shall succeed at tickling
the consciences of those who would
change the wild river's edge or alter
the untouched forests and bayous nearby.
My children tread the banks of long, spongy

baygalls filled with tangled, wild
thickets and haunting, shadowy brush arbors.

My children are the frolicking Autumn leaves
turning cartwheels in the frosty wind.
Their sand boxes are the spits and bars,
the long, looping mounds left abandoned
in the sharp river bends.
Briefly they pause play to lick
the cool sands piled high and white
like vanilla ice cream on
the dark chocolate shoreline.

Gooney woodpecker laughs and the frisky
chirps of frolicking squirrels
warmly greet me each morning at sunrise.
They, too, are my family.
Each night the owls, crickets and
bullfrogs sing quaint nursery rhymes
they have learned just for me.
Then my heart sings along and smiles.

Sometimes we sing in such harmony
that all who hear know we are of
the same joyful family.
They know this place
is a welcoming place
in which we all belong.

The Far Off Cries of Crows

Sometimes when the day is new and yawning
I hear the cries of circling crows.
Like wraiths without substance
their caws move through green shadowed treetops
on silent wings.
Only the sound of their shrill voices lets me know
they are coming.

Down the hillside hundreds of flattened spiders'
webs hang upside down like tiny parachutes
tangled in the tops of feathery weeds.
Strewn randomly across my un-mowed meadow,
they dangle at the mercy of morning's moist leavings.
With each soft breath of breeze they rise and fall,
prisoners of the wind wafting up
from the cool river's edge.

I hear water lazily dripping from the lip
of the tin roof.
It pleasantly plops
onto the worn out boards
of my wooden deck.
Brown, rustling leaves softly touch down
on the metal stairs
which lead upward
to solitude.

I have come here hoping for a rest
only to find that I am up before daylight
with pen and pad, anxious to get started.

I can do nothing but sit and listen to the crows
as they circle back and forth,
then around again.
They tell me to stop wasting my time
trying to figure out where the words will come from.
The words flow so well on my porch at sunrise.

Reflections on a Rooftop

My roof needed sweeping from
the aftermaths of several storms which
had passed over months before.
I had watched the mounded piles grow taller,
randomly deposited with the leftovers
from a harsh Winter we had miraculously survived.
I could not bring myself to climb up there
and deal with it.
Somehow my broom and rake seemed inadequate
to begin the task.
The work was high and slippery.
I felt dread when I imagined
myself braving those heights with just a
wooden ladder to elevate me and my tools.
A parachute jump seemed safer and more appropriate.

Two heavy limbs had fallen on the roof
during a hurricane: their omnipresence made me nervous.
Like eerie sentinels they seemed poised,
waiting for me, daring me to accost them.
Like wooden Sumo wrestlers they were intimidating,
large and unwieldy.
If I tangled with them I would be placing my life in peril.

I had done this task many times before.
The job was well above the ground, about 25 feet.
I knew that, should I fall, when I landed I would
break apart like a crumbling sawdust mannequin.
It took some time before, on rubbery legs, I
ascended the shaky wooden ladder.

I tightly clutched the broom and rake in my
feeble fist and began climbing to my doom.

I could have sworn I heard my ears pop
as I gingerly alighted on the roof's edge and surveyed
the corrugated metal surface for hidden dangers.
It was a pleasant Saturday morning and once I had gotten
up there, I took a deep breath and began to relax.
First to go were the large limbs I had fretted over.
Treading close to the roof's edge was intimidating.
I tried to ignore that looming boundary
of sure destruction and soon commenced a thorough
sweeping of my roof.
Thousands of tiny twigs and leaves had been dislodged
from the tops of lofty oaks, sweetgums,
beeches and wild persimmon trees.
Their various leavings were easy to differentiate.

A mountain of tiny scraps was interspersed
with a years-worth of discarded acorn caps,
bits of bark and the dregs of other seasons passed.
All these were lodged like little dams in the
corrugated grooves and channels of the metal roof.
This detritus, if ignored, could back up
the rain runoff and cause a worrisome leak
which might stain my newly painted kitchen ceiling.

How un-kept this roof has gotten, I thought
to myself.
I knew that it was my own fault.
I had taken my roof for granted.
That humble, sheltering structure which I had securely

slept beneath for more than two decades
was in sore need of my assistance.
Out of fear I had failed to inspect it properly.
By my neglect it had fallen into disorder.
My docile defender had endured my procrastinations,
patiently awaiting my selfishly denied attention.

A forgiving roof dreams of a bold champion
who will brave its heights and save its humble face.
A thorough warden of the estate would not have left
either a miscreant limb or an abandoned clump
of leaves behind to cause mischief.
Yet, my roof had never complained, never groaned
with the added mass of leaves and limbs
pressed down upon it.
It had not leaked in protest of my neglect.
My faithful roof had continued to protect me and mine,
to shield my mundane life even though its owner,
totally out of hand, had abandoned it to nature's
relentless onslaught and undeserved degradation.

Aggrieved by my own inaction, forced
to address the roof's unspoken grievances,
I cautiously crept onto its rusting surface
with humility and a broom and made my amends.
With as humble a voice as I could muster at that moment,
I promised that I would never let this happen again.
My roof tacitly agreed to continue doing its only work.
After all, a roof's only purposes are to guard a house's
contents and to remain indefinitely ignored.

Mowing as Dharma (2)

I wonder, do the great oaks complain about
not having struck a bargain with me and my lawnmower.
They are so old that they rarely produce
viable acorns which the squirrels, deer and
feral pigs hope to harvest.
If they could, would the oaks make the same
bargain that the persimmons made with Shiva?

Someone must decide what goes or stays.
Do they consult their sacred Stuti for advice?
How are the sweetgums at reading the astral signs?
They hold their leafy hands and arms high in puja.
I do not believe they have carefully considered the
uncertain futures of their progeny.

My lawnmower does not care.
It mows them all over with impunity.
Their Zombie seedlings will simply grow back
from headless stumps.

The weeds don't care, either.
Our native varieties are restless and relentless
in their competition with foreigner grasses
They spread out and thicken with each mowing.
Interlopers attempt to displace their
leafy adversaries, the natives mostly.
Always, the natives are in uprising in my yard.

A wealthy and generous River feeds them all,
persistently depositing rich silt
with semi-annual predictability.

Along with the floods come new plant seeds
which sprout and thrive for a season,
only to be replaced by something else
the next.

Each event represents another Brahman cosmos
filling and emptying its contents
so that a tenuous equilibrium may be achieved.
For a while my yard remains stable and
richly varied in negotiable species.
Then, the mower rolls out and
Shiva smiles again.

Young Hawks

A young hawk cries from somewhere up above,
hidden from view in a crowded, lofty canopy of green.
It searches for its family.
It hears no response from absent kin.
Now abandoned, it must seek its own answers.

Hawks know they must take wing and hunt, or perish.
They are hawks, lone hunters,
merciless and terrifying raptors.
Their young struggle to survive in the world,
dependent upon skills they were taught at a tender age.

Much the same, we teach our young in our own ways.
We send them out to become someone with special skills.
Sometimes they succeed, some fail, all struggle.
Struggle compels them to beseech a deaf humanity
which hears their cries, but rarely answers.

The cold wind blows and the rains pour down.
All their careful plans sometimes fail them.
When their strength is sorely tested,
finding answers can become a brutal contest.
They are forced to devise more suitable plans to survive.

Laying waste to their juvenile nests,
they explore new woods to hunt.
Courage unfurls their hidden wings again.
Grace will carry them on warmer currents,
to higher places, if they accept the dare.

Voyeurs

In the early morning hours
I watch the cool air slowly kissing the grass,
leaving its moist, lingering trace on stem and blade,
parched and panting,
out of breath in the heat of August.

Unrequited, the secret night has given
up and gone back home again,
accompanied by a bevy of consoling,
disappointed stars.
They have tired of being voyeurs
to the triste between the tall, enticing grass
and the early morning dew.

The lawn has grown too tall of late, uncut
since I last came to our cabin in the woods.
Built on stilts above a half-acre of wildness,
it is our bastion against accumulated cares and events.
I gratefully flee there for a time,
crawling up into the arms of a peaceful,
semi-secluded sanctuary.

Over the years most of our neighbors have given up.
They have permanently evacuated, fallen victims
of the numerous floods and hurricanes
which also seem to like coming here.
Their beloved homes were devastated,
as was ours, by consequence.
Or, perhaps by design: I often wonder which.

We have mostly put those events behind us.
We struggle to keep ahead of a relentless River
which is slowly, methodically claiming back
the land it wants for itself.
After all, it was Hers before it was ours.
She acknowledges no claims to this place but her own.
Heat and moisture are all grass needs to thrive here.
Sunshine is optional beneath the tall oaks and sweetgums.
Beebalm and marsh mallows bloom in the open bottom
lands.
Butterwort and milkweed blossoms feed the wild bees
which industriously mine all the fascia boards
of our old wooden house.
Next door ragweed and goldenrod grow chest high
up and down the slopes of a wide, dry slough,
abandoned, for the most part, by the river.

The Sabine River is a marvelous chef.
It regularly cooks up a rich and muddy
bouillabaisse, sometimes a gumbo.
Occasionally, the kettle boils over,
fattening the sandbars, reshaping the land.
With seasonal certainty it immerses all,
leaving behind diluvian delicacies
which the plants appreciate.

The names of the taller grasses I don't know.
They rage along the roadsides driving up here,
interspersed among the reeds and rushes, along with
sprouting American bamboo, which we call cane.
Long buried by the River, thick stands of cane
still thrive on its sandy shoulders.

The River recently scoured away several
inches of ancient loam from my property.
Patrolling canes have begun to march
up the edges of my driveway,
spears in hand, defiant of my lawnmower.
More protecting than menacing,
they take up positions like silent sentries
guarding the only path in and out.

They see everything that passes, but say nothing
to challenge the squirrels and armadillos
which root around in the yard, tearing up the sod,
burying acorns and searching for grubs, respectively.
Demotions are in order.
Off with their traitorous heads, I say.
Treacherous cane's allegiance to me
is temporal at best.
They serve no higher purpose than the humble
role I demand of them; their unwavering loyalty.

A green army masses and like some warrior king
protecting his territory I continue to
mercilessly mow down all challengers.
While I am still able, as long as the River
allows it, I will continue to come here
to rest, to work and to marvel.
Ours is a cold war with long periods of détente.
Each side earnestly wishes to control outcomes.
Only one holds true power.

The River ebbs and flows,
shows restraint for a time.
Its forces are forever in onslaught.
An ever vigilant River bivouacs its troops
on the borders of my yard,
quietly waiting and watching.
It patiently plans new campaigns,
overwhelming and impossible to predict.
I plan to marshal my forces and
keep an adequate supply of gasoline handy,
just in case.

Nature Holds Us

Nature holds its knowledge in a clenched fist.
The last great mysteries of science will always
be those discovered and explained by an
enigmatic Nature reluctantly giving up its secrets.
We owe our being to this force above all forces.

Mankind prevails by testing the limitations and
boundaries which the natural world has politely erected.
We never conquer it.
We only utilize its parts for our own needs.
We are a part of it as much as it is a part of us.

Nature seeks to have power over us just as much as we
seek to change it.
Each time we influence rivers to flow the way we want or
dig canals, or build housing complexes over swampland
we must consult Nature first or disasters happen.
Floods occur which dams were not built to hold back.
Canals drain the tidal swamplands which were meant to protect
fragile coastal marshes from erosion's adverse effects.
Housing complexes bring Nature to our doorsteps,
raw and untamed, and Nature has teeth.

Each time we want to change something about Nature,
if we do not try to make our best deal with it,
fully knowing its habits and tendencies,
the limitations it places on our technologies
will be borne out in many more disasters.

We are pitted against the greatest force
in the Universe.
Perhaps it is the Universe as we know it.

Perhaps Nature should not be so much considered
a thing we are in competition with
as it is a constantly changing force that
is put into place to help us survive.
What would our algorithms then predict?

The Honeymoon: Newer Sacred Mythologies

Floating fog frequently takes away my view of
the reliable River which graces my back yard's
scenic environ most mornings.
The world wakes up wrapped in soupy curtains
made of dew drops.

Summer heat has made the
oak tree leaves and limbs perspire.
Vine bordered sloughs sag,
heavily hung with dripping decorations
carelessly left out after last night's merriment.

Joined and joyfully wed were
the Starry Sky groom and the Laughing River bride.
She trailed her veil behind her and covered
the world in translucent whiteness.
Her exuberance threatened
to overflow her banks.

The couple smiled and waved as they quickly passed
through the brush arbor of their verdant wedding chapel.
They smoothly flowed along at a steady clip,
enamored with each other, intertwined.
They meandered and bubbled all night long,
carelessly in love.

They will honeymoon down by the Gulf of Mexico,
gather seashells and lazily strew driftwood logs
like garlands on all the strands and shorelines.

They will pass a blissful summer
spawning hurricanes and waterspouts,
playing masters of the tides.

They will compete with the jealous moon for dominance
over the waters and the seasons till Fall
finds them bored and restless to leave again.
The crabbers and the shrimpers will be the
last to return in their beat up fishing boats
to claim elusive catches from the marsh lined bays
at the River's mouth.
The happy couple will relax somewhere in the Caribbean,
at carnival until next summer rolls around,
when their yearly sacred wedding vows
are again renewed.

Relic

Ocean employ your roaring, gurgling voice.
Tell me the number of my days
You patiently count
Grain by precious grain
Falling, ever falling.

Waves tumble and scrape me clean of rust.
I am no jewel in the rough
Sand and surf polish, then buff
My lifeless body till I am renewed
A smooth perfection, such perfection.

Then I shall have life again, a curious trinket
Caught between a child's pudgy fingers
Played with contentedly on a crowded beach
With dream castles standing at my feet
Made of sand, shifting sand.

Dunes build me a barrow wide and deep
White and high and skyward piled
Fit for this fallen King of the dust
All flesh and bone now vanquished by time
Meant to rule no more, never more.

Rains seep down to my buried hiding place
Fill the sand casting secreted below
My calcified body lies deftly deposited there
Pressed and hardened, turned to new stone in time
For inquisitive fingers to seek, eagerly seek.

Waters millennia hence in no order or force of will
From newer stones you will give birth to me again
New formed differently than the old me I knew
Glistening and wet behind the ears with your birth dews
A castaway orphan of the tides washed up, washed clean.

Mother Ocean cradle your awkward wayward son
Come to rest now upon your rocky bosom
What matter how long or brief his stay will be.
All will arrive to become like him someday
Again with you, once again with you.

Timeless and temporal, then lifeless
Then living then dying, then living are we.
Beginning then ending, born again and again
Ever perished ever completed, ever changed.
Waters course over me till I am new, ever new.

The Stillness of the Morning

Morning falls in upon itself
in deafening vacuum.
Not a cricket or a bird
is chirping.
The silence of the night
rubs elbows with the day's
gentler stirrings.

Dawn is born dreaming in colors,
entwined with shadows in the tall grass,
freshly bathed and swaddled,
glistening with new dewdrops on its brow.

Hear the quiet sighs of sycamore souls.
A friendly breeze tousles
their slender white branches,
festooned with dying leaves, just trading hues
of yellow for chestnut brown.
The season's turning is upon them.
Their marble white trunks stand
like tall columns holding up
the pale blue roof of the world.
The scent of Winter hangs in the air.
Soon will come the expected transformation
before a long sleep.
A cold, grey wolf pack called Winter
trails its quarry, ruthlessly devouring all
that is green and growing.

The stoic beeches stand and shiver,
their rust and copper clad
twigs rattle with anticipation.
River birches bring out their gold wrappings as
raiding Autumn greedily plunders their leafy coffers.
Harsh November winds mercilessly maraud.
Rugged raiders without conscience,
they soon strip bare the willows and maples,
violently casting aside their maroon and gold tunics.
Shamed and silenced, the other trees stand by
watching the heartless onslaught.
Wooden trunks are callously laid bare
to frost, cold winds and pounding rains
that always ensue on this, the edge of Winter.

The trees will ultimately submit
to Autumn's ruthless ravishing.
Hard-hearted Winter will tromp its way
across the high heavens.
The steadfast stars will look down
upon the weeping trees.
With sparkling solace they will shine
their bright promises,
hanging forever fixed against
the hollow, desperate darkness.
You will endure, they whisper
with a twinkle in their ever shining eyes,
You will endure.

Part Two

Love's
Blind
Shambling

If I were not so blind to the obvious I would never find myself lonely, much less alone.

Jerry Lovelady

My Two-Dimensional Refrigerator Universe

The living and the dead vie for elbow room
on my two dimensional refrigerator universe.

Spanning six decades of love and sorrow,
their faces and bodies are warped and
compressed into two dimensional form
by time and memories.

Their still frame eyes laugh,
posed corny smiles glow,
ever elated and grouped alongside
warmer images of happy people hugging, holding,
supporting a pleasant past.

Both knowns and anonymous share
space in sepia and grey splendor
sprung from snap shots taken in a
black and white world, now encased
in crinkled, paper bordered edges.

Timeless frames are filled with frozen grins,
gleaming white teeth, perfected hairdos.

Loving great-aunts and uncles, cousins and old
friends are captured securely by magnets
which vertically pin them to the
gleaming white door of the freezer compartment.

They hang lovingly suspended in better times,
clutched hard to other old memories

which will last long after we are wasted dust,
when the Junk Man takes our universe away.

Infant, to toddler, to teen, to adult
relatives ripen from image to flattened image.
Intimate decades are projected, truncated, condensed,
lovingly captured in the act
of celebrating their vibrantly lived lives.

The posed old homestead recounts its own
snow covered universe within a universe
as pale white winter days are reconstituted
on the icebox.

It's August, but the snow never melted.
Over a thick blanketed front yard milieu
the immortal snowman still proudly reins.

Fir boughs hang evergreen and fresh
on a weathered screen door.
Ribbons flutter, suspended in the absent breeze:
red satin streamers vainly attempt to wave.

Presents fill all the spaces
beneath a fresh cut tree, hung with strings
of popcorn and real candy canes.
Grandma in her housecoat and curlers
wears a knowing smile.

Crawling puppies and tots scramble, gleefully
unaware that the camera's roving eye has
snared them, marooned them into a

short lived immortality,
stuck to refrigerator doors.

Excitement seems to seep through the cracks
in space and time as the images pass
one by one through sentimental eyes,
across great expanses into the vacuum
of our melancholic hearts.

Onward go those memories
to other broad universes
we keep hidden away inside us,
always searching for another place
to light and make us smile again.

Waiting, Hoping, Watching

Waiting, hoping, watching,
I can do nothing without you.

Attached, anchored, melded,
cut your finger, I bleed.

Moan, cry out, epithets flow.
I curse all who would offend you.

The mirror holds only your reflection.
Where have I gone?

Who am I?

Stolen Moment (1)

I
stole an eager kiss that lingered
  breathless sighs were loudly bursting
  behind curtains in your closet
  when your lover was nearby.
Fire of fantasy's fulfillment
  in such ecstasy kept quiet.
Then we both regained composure
  as we strolled into the den.

You
stole a glance in my direction
  when they filled our clinking glasses
  at the banquet in your honor
  as the toasters took their turns.
Our eyes met and you were with me
  once more hidden in that closet
  sharing one more stolen moment;
  no one else knew we were there.

Waiting in the Moonlight

Whom is it you seek?
Is it I?

Your eyes inquire,
your face inspires.
You pose and sigh.

Where did you find
that flower
so prominently placed
in your platinum hair?

Did your lover
place it there
before my arrival
this late hour?

My Idol

Day bows in worship of its light
radiantly posed in her satin night shift.
Honey drips from her rose petal lips,
slightly parted by a smile.

Divine perfume she hides
in an eider down bosom.
Each delectable whiff is like
candy to my senses.
To capture this vision
is my preternatural longing.
This drowsy deity is my bronzed goddess.
She lies hopelessly resplendent
on her sun-kissed strand,
a royal wayfarer to some sandy shore.

When disappointment crinkles my idol's brow
the honey sours on her sharp edged tongue.
Her serrated words rend
my flesh and bone devotion.
Her laser gaze tears gaping holes in my
mantel of pious steadfastness.
That is when my lovely statue's feet crack open
to reveal her claw tipped toes
that peek through the ruined casting.

My pleasure boat is capsized
in the unexpected gale which follows.
I swim for my life, foundering among
schools of hungry sharks.

Soft words may console a wounded heart,
but words do nothing to erase bad memories.
Lurid billows threaten today's contentment.
Over time the clouds will dissipate to reveal
my idol, mud in hand,
reshaping herself to her own liking.
No one may possess her.
None can predict her whims.

A true force of Nature,
she drives men before her,
binding us hopelessly
to her newly wrought image.
Maddened by devotion,
we dutifully worship her,
against all will to, otherwise
do what we would.

Bring Me No More Sorrows

Spare me your shrill laments about
your virtue in the grey morning light
when night obstinately
refuses to depart.
When sleep refrains from closing
my tired, restless eyes.
When no dreams are ushered forth
to dance with abandon
across my mind's dormant dancefloor.

Please pay me no more lip service.

Well intended as your words
might be, they serve to placate only you.
Each and every foul sentence you coldly serve
heartlessly assaults me.
I made vain attempts at forgetting all the
small worries I have about trusting you.
I trust you less each time this happens.

Send me no more rainbows
for my pale horse to leap over
as we trot away toward the horizon.
As I fade away by degree
from your shining memory of me,
try not to laugh.
Your picture window will cloud over
the dusky grey hills in the background
till my silhouette vanishes
from your vision
forever.

Just a Spark

Does the glow of love remain here
like the warmth of tender kisses
placed on sorrowed cheeks left pining
in their darkest night on earth?

Just a breath of comfort left near
for a heart so cold and distant
from the fires of love eternal
cast away to cringe in pain.

In the darkness you will not fear.
No dark shadows can assault you.
No force nature wields can harm you
nor will come to cause you grief.

Think of me and I shall be there
with these arms made just to warm you.
Till your fears have fled forever:
then you'll know that you are loved.

These Are My Excesses

Do you remember the time I captured the moon
and placed the stars in a row for you?
That was just for fun.
You made me mend that rent in the heavens
so that the stars would not have a place
to hide away all day.
I was so proud of myself, but
you said that you could do better.

With the cool nothingness of your brown eyes you
effortlessly wrangled together all the constellations.
You transfixed them somehow.
They seemed captured by your magical gaze alone.
You paralyzed them with that same empowered look
I never was able to shake.
If you had thrown me a dog biscuit I would have
gratefully lain at your feet and chomped.
One glimpse of those eyes and I was
hopelessly captured.

Then, you shaped all those stars into a pentagram.
That was impressive, I must admit.
It was quite a letdown, though, when I
figured out you wanted more than that.
It was not enough for you just to peer aimlessly
into our vague future together, greedily
clutching at each other every night.
I felt completely satisfied
happily living in the exciting moments we shared.

I found myself resting on the bottom of your private fjord
staring up at the glaciers nestled in your eyes.
Like a sleepy sea trout I waited,
stilled and motionless.
When your attractive bait floated
my way I rose to capture it.
Then came the steel hook reward
which lodged in my begrudging jawbone.
Small wonder I ended up another trophy
hung over your fine fireplace mantel.

I remember your touch was velvet and chamois.
Soft madness etched filigree runes
into my rough hide.
With a peacock's feather you traced
scrumptious tickles of your maddening
intentions on my heaving chest.
My body understood you:
no need for further explanations.
I read the runes and gasped for breath.

You kept smiling down at me as
star fire flashed from your hollow eyes.
Arm in arm we rose up to the boats
gently floating on the stilled water above.
All the other drunken partiers
somehow seemed to know your name.
A giddy wind blew through my mind's open window
as I tried in vain to guess your thoughts.
Intrigue and frustration ran amok as I speculated.
You smiled the smile of a naughty saint
who knew all the answers I was seeking,
but mirthfully refused to reveal them.

Or a poker player who just pulled off a bluff,
all in, that won the largest pot of the night.
With a smirk you raked all the stars into a pile,
kissed God on the lips, and
vanished with everything.

Oh, Queen

No claim, my Queen, do I presume
to stake upon your precious time.
A vast realm of fortuitous holdings
captivates your divine attention.
Unruly subjects grovel;
unhappy duchies grumble.
You placate or subjugate them at your whim.
Command: your will is ours, my sovereign.
As I bow lower the knap of your
fine Kashan rug
tickles my bushy eyebrows.

Your crown, prominently bejeweled
with your previous, grand accomplishments
tilts slightly over one glaring,
midnight eye.
Your razor tongue rakes
your servant's stubbly face,
acrimony for lather.
Please spare me more unearned derision
which you regularly heap upon
this, your hapless devotee.

You raise the heavy jeweled scepter
with aggrandized flair.
It was designed to mimic a killing mace,
meant for maiming transgressors.
Delicately, ceremoniously you extend
your authority high above submissive heads.
Would that it made you feel loved,

respected, all powerful and possessed of true
authority, when it only serves to command fear,
insecurity and despair among your subjects.
Which is no good replacement for their love.

Thrown Away

Would you toss me away just like that,
knowing what you know about me, and I about you?
No one is ever really finished with
the other when we say we are.
Love just lies in wait like a friendly Ninja
to ambush our hearts again.

As I stepped away from the red flags
which you erected around yourself
you backed away from my barbed wire defenses.
Your cold, regretful shoulders were turned askew.
Both of us wished we could vanish.
Then our eyes met and in that brief glance
we knew we wanted each other again.

That's when I began wishing for more.
For the kind of more that never has to end.
Sometimes cool reason persuades heated passions
to capitulate.
Our first emotional upheaval ended poorly,
my back turned toward your back.
The night before we cuddled like
two spoons in the drawer.

Tonight I see unhappy tears seeping from the corners
of your downcast eyes and I grieve.
My face betrays the uncertainty hiding in me.
My intuition senses cunning emotional bombs
which you left behind for me to stumble over.
Like hidden IED's they are precisely timed
to go off as soon as you stealthily leave the room.

I stare into space and worry about
what will become of us after Love
leaves us behind like bloody casualties.
I don't know how to perform CPR
for this kind of injury.

Fickle Love wears its body armor to parties.
It always escapes the fray unscathed
to wistfully roam wherever it pleases,
oblivious to any freeway pileup of emotions
it will eventually create in other
lives it carelessly touches.

Innocently, the party goers will continue
to entertain the odd idea that
this sort of devastation
will never happen to them.

Lover's Bridge

We left our lock in Paris
on a bridge over the Seine.
We latched it to the railing,
on its body wrote our names.

The key we tossed right then and there
in the waters deep and cold,
with several thousand others whose
good fortunes would be told.

The "Lover's Bridge" they call it.
Local folks are heard to say,
If you leave your lock upon it
your true love will always stay.

Though I'm not fond of legends
I believe that this one's true.
That lock's still latched to my heart
on a bridge from me to you.

More Than Enough Love

When I found you still up crying late one night
while Dad was working out of town
I did not know what was wrong or
how to comfort you.
You pulled it together and just told me
to go to sleep.
You hid your pain and I knew
something was wrong, but I let it go.

Into the wee hours your typewriter endlessly
tapped on our kitchen table.
You practiced the lost language of shorthand;
scribbled cyphers jotted onto cryptic paper scraps
littered the floor in the morning.
You always had lunch money handy for us,
though you often did without yours.
You reared six children practically by yourself
juggling night school and family for years.
All of us owed you more respect than we gave.

One Spring morning you bought some baby chicks,
along with a dozen varieties of vegetable seeds
from the local feed store.
You brought them home determined to raise
those Rhode Island Reds for eggs and meat.
The hungry possums got the eggs.
Clever chicken hawks made off with the hens.
To offset the losses you simply planted a few
more rows of lima beans.

That cold December we went into the woods
to cut a scrawny Christmas tree.
Together we struggled to drag it back home.
We strung popcorn on its slender boughs,
an angel cut out of colored paper
graced its lopped off top.

Oranges and Brazil nuts filled
our tube sock stockings
hung with care above the butane space heater.
A pair of underwear and one toy each were
our only gifts that Christmas.
I did not find a gift under the tree for you.

Hot cocoa warmed our souls those
cold winter nights.
Popcorn or homemade doughnuts thrilled us
on rainy weekends spent loafing around the house.
Visits to the doctor when I was ill
turned into drugstore outings for comic books
and chicken salad sandwiches on toast.
Sometimes you bought me model airplanes
which I glued together as soon as we got home.
How I loved getting sick.

You always told us to be grateful for
everything we had, as little as it was sometimes.
We were happy with life.
It gave plenty of love to all of us.
One evening I sneaked a peek at your poetry,
which you tried to hide from your heathen brood
in a shoe box stashed high on your closet shelf.

I quickly realized that it was marvelous writing and
instantly resolved to write poetry like yours someday.

Joyful tunes filled our little house at Christmas,
even when the years were not so good to us.
If I was down, I could always look to you
to put a happy song in my heart.
You showed me that I could write my own story.
That was the greatest gift you could
give to a young man like me.
That was more than enough love for a lifetime.

For the Love of Words

I have no greater purpose in life
than to be a lover of words
which suit me well
in all they tell of men
and things not so mortal
or so vain.

Whatever one may say aloud
is not nearly as eternal
as a world built by
strong words laid
in a line, winding on,
stacked atop one-another,
hop-scotching across a leaf
of remnant, cellulose scrap,
or thickly stuffed into a dusty,
leather bound tome.
All are the same,
both mundane and extraordinary.
Even these lines are wordy particles of a whole
which changes its meaning at
every pen stroke.

In each simple word there
is a life, timeless and immortal,
meaningless and ignored, hallowed or derided.
When new words are laid down
there, too, am I again
mastering the pen
which wants to write its head.
Reined in for a time, it collects the words.

What needs to be said is
cemented to an eager page,
its greater purpose realized at last.

Part Three

A

Rhapsody

for Contrite Hearts

To avoid the pain of living we would remake ourselves into Gods. Fortunately, we are not capable of such remarkable feats. To make up for our inadequacies we pretend we are better than others. Without love, all who think they are wealthy find that they are actually the poorest.

J. Lovelady

The Surfers

They come back from the ocean in the fading light.
Caught up in the hissing effervescence like organ pipes
in crescendo, the surfers desert a house of perfect
sand and dazzling sun.

They leave reverently in small throngs
having uttered vespers under contrite breath.
Worship services have concluded for the day
in the temple of their new religion.

Up the crumbling hillside they reluctantly trudge
lugging their magic carpets under tired arms.
They have paddled them out and back many times
on the long haul to and from shore.

Old and young alike have a satisfied look,
quiet smiles on far seeing, reflective faces
having had epiphanies in the jade green waters
of the California coastline.

One by one, or in pairs they dutifully make their way
to their jalopies and upscale cars, trucks and vans
for the long ride home, or a short one for those
who chose to take up residence
close by these holy places,
nestled next to the sacred swells and breakers.

Each morning the oceans' bells ring out
from their shining cathedrals in the bay.
The devout answer the call to services
as low rumbles fill the cool morning air.

The waves boom their sermons from a churning,
curling surf as worshipers of all ages heed the call.

They deeply breath in the sea salt incense
till it bursts their happy lungs,
till the disquiet of their lives rushes out
with the ebbing tide.
Till, solemn and pleasantly tired,
they reverently kneel in the sacred sands
as the gentler light of the evening fades away.

Pleasurable sensations buoy their quieted minds
as all cares and rituals are carelessly discarded
at the end of another grateful day alive.
Their cathedral is the wild and churning ocean.
All are welcome here.

Such Is Poetry

So much has been said
of why poetry is created.
Life as we know it,
are yet to know of it, or
never even considered knowing
all succinctly described
in the shorthand of poetry.

In a thing called poetry
a few short sentences are written,
meant to express what whole chapters
might be penned to explain.
Incompleteness, on purpose;
enigmatic by design,
cryptically sacred, is poetry.

Tender hands write rich histories,
almost a religion to some scholars.
Captured snapshots to be ogled,
dissected, fawned over,
marveled at and revered,
forever festooned on common paper.

The bits and pieces
of lifetimes stored on fragile leaves
wait only for the lovers
of words to drop in
and drag them out again.

A book opens,
feet prop up and rest.
The eye and the intellect

discern the winding way to peace
lovingly threaded into written lines.
They use those words to mend their troubled souls.

Silent Night

Wide sky moon blushes,
blinks her lone, silvery eye.
Her mascara is running all over the sky.
Blue and gray eye shadows have come and gone
without fanfare.
Inky black shading spills from horizon
to blurred horizon
strewn with sparkling remnants of worlds
and shards of far flung yesterdays.
In red shift some remain
utterly unreachable,
fugitive suns deserting us forever.

Desolate darkness has seized
the eastern slopes of the mountain.
Its black, hulking silhouette
has devoured the emerging stars
leaving a cone shaped bite
in the pin wheeling universe.
The music of the heavens plays on
as celestial melodies float on the breeze
dispersed among the twinkling stars.

A haunting rendition of "Silent Night" begins
to play on ebon keys as apparitions murmur
softly in a darkened, sleepy eyed desert
which tugs at star splashed covers and
rolls over to catch a few
more precious winks
before Night's lonely repertoire
has finally finished.

Communion Wine

A jewel backed hummingbird patiently sits
her tiny clutch of eggs
in a sheltered nest beneath the broad leaves
of a giant tapioca tree.
From my balcony overhang
two stories up I watch her quiet vigil
as she listens for hatching sounds.
All she owns in this world
are two diminutive eggs and gravity,
which she has delightfully mastered.

Born in the salt spray and sunshine
she proudly surfs the airwaves,
a true west coast native.
She hovers effortlessly,
her aerobatic prowess the envy
of Harrier jump jets.
On the wing she is majesty incarnate,
defender and protector of her queendom,
sovereign over flowers and ferns.

She bows to no one in her iridescent,
finely feathered raiment.
Her mossy nest is her throne.
The warm, red earth her richly woven carpet.
A cloud dappled mural hangs above her.
Each day she daintily sips royal nectars
made by gentler gods
for her communion wine
as her court genuflects
to Her Majesty,
the Queen of California.

The Eastern Side of the Mountains

In the high desert stand tall mountains
which block encroaching luminescence
of western cities, guarding the eastern skies.
Voluptuous Night dresses up,
blinks a billion silvery eyes.
She comes out to view us,
to tease and wink at us
and flirt with passing
meteors and comets.

Richly attired and brightly
sequined, the stars arrive.
Their twinkling bodies boldly pinned
to flowing black velvet dresses.
The evening sky wears a low slung gown
tightly stretched over the pale,
sandy figure of the Earth.
Her outfit is sublime
and she shamelessly flaunts it.

Pulsing codes flash back and forth
as twinkling sentinels keep watch for
the intruder moon who might rise up to murder
the noble procession of distant luminaries.
Dancing bodies punctuate the perpetual blackness.
Whirling quasars hang like mirror balls.
Strident syncopations announce the approach
of visiting planetary celebrities.

Mars dominates in his angry red blazer,
followed by Jupiter and Saturn,

overarching, hulking and suave gas giants.
They strut about slowly as they mingle.
They prefer brighter conversationalists,
changing partners frequently.
Ursa Major and Minor turn do-si-dos with
Orion, Sagittarius, Gemini and Scorpio.
Together they blithely wheel about the edges
of a visible vortex hub
we earthlings call the Milky Way.
A small pinwheel in the cosmos,
our galaxy innocuously hangs out
in a mostly empty part of our universe.

Heavenly bodies quizzically chuckle
while we wonder back at them
trying to understand colossal events
which they begrudgingly conceal.
Events which we pretend to happen in the now,
but transpired decades, centuries,
or eons ago.

What mirth we must spawn in the heavens.
Constant postulations,
contradictory observations,
dire predictions, all to no avail.
The Heavens will do what they will
and we will wonder at it all
without clues, in the dark,
on the eastern side of the mountains.

Godlike and Unafraid

I sit at the kitchen table,
godlike and unafraid
while the house rattles and shakes
with each frightful percussion.

My cats scurry to the safety of the den,
attempting to hide under loose couch skirts,
which they believe will protect them
from discovery by nasty Mr. Thunder.

They quiver and quake with each anvil strike.
Their tiny brains do not comprehend
converging pressure gradients.

Unshaken and courageous during such events,
I compose lengthy letters to Thor
proclaiming a truce in my present onslaught
against fabricated deities who
purportedly control the weather down here
from somewhere up there.

In the meantime, I keep my head down and try
to deftly duck his lightning bolts.

Sky Regatta

The sky's prism is cracking.
A rainbow is fracturing, a waterfall of
       leaking, truncated colors, spilling,
       pouring pell-mell over boulders embedded in
       a white rapid swirl of turbulence that is the sky.
The clouds have hauled down their answering pendants.
A white water regatta of sunbeams whips up the waves
       in a race down the rapids
       on a grey hued dash toward
       the shrinking horizon.

Jubilant green giants standing on the shore
       sway with excitement.
They raise their arms in praise for the bold contestants,
       their high heads used for worshiping,
       no knees to bend in prayer, their
       playful spirit wishes flow
       to the netherworld
       where patient ears and eyes observe
       through hidden clefts in time and space.
Who will win is already known,
       only waiting for outcomes
       to be exuberantly confirmed
       by curious observers.

Unperturbed by Current Events

Unperturbed by current events,
I hold up useless lines I have invented
so that I may brave inclement
consequences intruding into my life.
Bleak forecasts are unsettling, at best.
No one else is prepared to save me
from an incomprehensible future.

In this house, which serves as my buffer
against powers greater, by far,
than my own, I often hole up and worry.
Different winds blow and rattle my confidence.
I am painfully aware of the
unimaginably dominant powers which assault me
here and now, yet keep far enough away
from my limited perception to seem unreal.
My security is imperfect, lasting only
as long as life allows me to believe I am safe.

Winds bend over the tree tops of my finances.
Thunder vibrates the window panes of my
meager real estate holdings.
Car bombs obliterate far off hospitals and schools
as I passively watch from my living room.
All current events now seem like expected chaos.
Lightning repeatedly etches the skyline
with enough current to electrify
the whole country for a week.
Yet, we still have not learned how to
save it for a snowy day when
inevitably, all the lights will go out.

I calmly sit and daydream in blessed detachment.
My pen scratches a few archaic symbols
of civilized vocabulary onto leftover wastepaper
leaflets, cut half sheets provided by my devoted wife
and stapled together for my hand written musings.
Scraps become dutifully saved heirlooms
in the hope that someone will eventually
read and enjoy these beautifully written rants.

I persistently maintain
the vain hope that my words
will make good sense to someone, someday.
I tell my cats it will be alright
as they nervously huddle under the couch skirts
hiding from eminent disasters they constantly perceive.
Still, they choose not to listen to reason.
Instead, trusting their own council,
they pray to me for mercy and protection.
These blessings I would gladly give
if only I possessed them for myself.

Modern Astronomy

The Moon braided the Sun's hair
with her own this morning.
The Sun's golden locks streaked
a pale patchwork sky.
The Moon's silver tresses trailed
the softly falling twilight
like silver threads traced
over the bare white shoulders
of the sleeping mountains.

Flirtatious Venus, a flashing,
gaudy, sequin of a woman, swiftly
rode her chariot forth
through the dim lit heavens.
She coyly winked at Jupiter
as he passed low on an Autumnal horizon.
Ursa Major and Scorpio at once locked gazes.
They commenced to sway a slow Samba
which ended with the Big Dipper.

Saturn the Age Bringer
briefly joined the gyre,
retiring forthwith to his bed
for a sacrosanct slumber below
an abrupt western horizon.
A wrathful Mars tromped onto
the edge of the crowded sky
in the wee hours,
petulant and embittered.

Like a gruff bouncer
he gleefully expelled
all the tipsy merrymakers.
Night slammed its doors shut as
an effervescent Dawn arrived
bringing rain.

Something Wicked Comes

Tree limbs clap and clatter
in the grasp of a gusty gale.
Twigs crash 'round and tumble down--
to the soggy ground they sail.
Porch boards creak and shudder
from the weight of a pressing wind
as early winter's onslaught starts,
just before the snows begin.

The twilight dreary times arrive
with chills we loathe to linger.
When Jack Frost nips the tender tips
of our toes or an exposed finger.
Time to bundle in a cozy place
with a crackling fire side blaze.
Warm blanket and a favorite book
with which the mind might laze.

The crouching house is pummeled by
bombasts from the howling winds.
Cold sleet pelts fragile window panes.
Tin roof rolls like a snare drum's dins.
All earth seems clenched in clamminess
as night gales still, the roaring dumbed.
No other sounds to break the silence:
portents that something wicked comes.

Great Waves of Change

Great waves of change punish the shore.
Loud forces shout, a distant roar.
They clash and scar their confined banks
in staggered rows and countless ranks.

A cunning voice draws ever near
with strident words that reach my ear.
Bold sounds of hope are loudly said
which calm my fevered, worried head.

Nothing is lost, but only changed
as Earth is once more rearranged.
The sea and sky will never rest.
They shape this world as they see best.

Solace to the Blind

Blind orbs rotate aimlessly out of focus
in the dull, asphyxiating darkness.
Hollow wheezes escape thick breathed lungs,
labored and strained from inhaling black,
molasses vapors from a smoldering night before.

The silent telephone ridicules
all the wasted keening.
Like unwanted visitors
pitiful whimpers proceed with impunity.
Then muffled moans of regret drop by
unbidden and unwanted.
Last to arrive are large, wet tears
which feebly fall upon grief flushed cheeks.

Morning peeks through the window shades
at un-rumpled pillows,
makes fun of a still made bed,
which holds no promise in it for sleeping.
Twilight memories mock
the warmth of yesterday's glowing,
still radiating from
an empty elbow's crook.
Fugitive Love plays
dilettante to loneliness again.

Resolve desperately claws its way
through bulwarks of self-pity.
Clods of darkness cling deftly
to its coattails.

Disheartened Resolve has slammed the door shut,
stalked off mumbling epithets to itself.
Regret, with dire loneliness for company,
becomes a solace for the blind,
left together to loudly wail and gnash their teeth.

This Pile of Rocks and Splinters

Come into this church,
this dividing house of souls.
Its walls were rent from stones of the earth.
Its frame splintered from great forests
of the world, put to this holier purpose;
a gathering place for the lost.

The lame are called to haltingly walk
through its tall cast bronze doors.
The deaf stand by so patiently and
feign listening to long sermons about
the poor and the hungry.
Earnest litanies are passionately said here,
spoken by modern day saints and martyrs
to a restless, listless conclave of sinners,
whether they need to hear them or not.

The prideful will kneel in the high arched apse
in front of the bloody altar God gave them
to trade in their sorrows for joy.
They cast down their fortunes at the feet of the Lord,
generous bribes offered for his saving grace,
unable or unwilling to give away
a little bit of love to others
less fortunate than they have been.

Hand down the hallowed holy book
all mouths fear to utter against.
Tongues will loosen; witnesses will slander
what they know about the truth.

Written in blood, many will deny
What pertains to them on any given Sunday.

The blind will claim to see the light
which stubbornly refuses to shine only for them.
In this pile of rocks and splinters
which we call church, a most sacred place,
all are most welcome to visit.

Part Four

Simple Songs
of
Meager
Self-Awareness

Being self-aware can be very tricky. If I am not self-aware I run the risk of seeming unsophisticated. If I am self-aware, I may be labeled conceited. It is a very risky business to know one's self.

J. Lovelady, 2021

Oh, Happy Day!

When I was a little boy I pretended
things that frightened me
would vanish
if I simply closed my eyes
and wished them away.

I matured.
I learned to avert my gaze
when confronted with disturbing
often embarrassing events.
I also came to believe that
if I didn't see things
or
ignored what I did see
then those things
would not have
real consequences
for me later on.

I became an adult.
My slightly open mind's eye
blinked tightly shut.
Oh, happy day!
With eyes wide open
I had learned the power
of outright denial
to remove the sting
of knowing absolutely
anything
about the truth.

A Golden Leaf

I watched a golden leaf
that spiraled to the ground
in summer not so sear,
the weather not so dry.
In fact, the air was moist:
the rains had newly ceased.
Fall was a distant scene
waiting for my fresh eyes to spy.

A golden leaf's time passed.
It was not due to end.
I'm left to think that things
must have much shorter terms
than I was made to know.
Is death a mortal end
or staged impermanence
so I might feel at ease when dead?

Of all these mysteries vast,
the greatest to the least,
what are we when we die
seems direst of all news.
Memories shape my days,
obscurely seen or dreamt.
Through each dim season's change
I wander perplexed even now.

Another leaf has fallen from the tree.
I cannot help but wonder, is that me?

Resisting Change

How dear a life I have to freely live,
my errors and my sins yet to forgive.
Atonement for a past less than contrite
hides behind flimsy curtains in plain sight.

The course is set to guide my feet anew
unburdened of all guilt for what I do.
My star forever pointing to its North
waits only for my courage to creep forth.

If change is needed while I take a breath
let change arrive before my sudden death.
Better to change than stay that same old me
who anguished over what might never be.

It is the now which calls to me so sweet.
Days dreamt and precious memories replete
with idleness and surety of peace
which waits in every moment's fresh release.

This is the Nature of Grief

Grief is a time wrenching line in the sand
I draw with a blood soaked finger
unsure of myself and weary
of my crusading
internal battles
while cohorts rage
year in and year out.

Struggles and loss are
surreptitiously conjured.
Unresolved conflicts persist.
Un-kept promises stubbornly
refuse to give way to
blessed thoughtlessness.

Unwieldy solutions burrow out
from under my safely stowed conscience
to intentionally stagnate me
more than to offer any hope.

Grief suppresses the recognition
of its own image cast in
a tarnished mirror and hastily traded
for multiple short lived
scenarios of peace.

Greif demands many immediate
small sacrifices.
First to go are my personal freedoms
abandoned for the greater good
followed by abdication of most

well established and
acceptable social standards
for the same reasons.

Deliberate oppression of joy ensues.
All this must happen so that others
may enjoy their hollow peace at my expense.
For the sake of good hygiene I will burn
the bodies of the fallen
in the town square of my reputation.

This is the nature of grief:
To ever wear a smile while
my brain is rudely dissected
by my ruthless opponents.

As my peace of mind angrily tromps away
perennial losers will bankrupt
my serenity label me a
cowardly traitor misanthropic
heretic and build a new scaffold
in my honor.

These are the times when I
stealthily slip off.
Just before my remorseless conscience
comes with armed guards looking
to drag me away
to be re-educated
again.

Free Range Love

No one arrives in this world
brimming with hope.
Anticipating others to act in ways different
than I expected them to was something I
could not imagine happening to me.
I was good at putting those expectations
on everyone else, though.
My intellect bound me to all lost causes
with ropes of hope.
Why was it so difficult for me
to just believe that what I wanted
out of life would eventually come to pass?
I still do not know the answer.

When my calendar turns to this time of year
I tell myself for the millionth time,
This time it will all come true.
Love will land next to me
to make its nest and stay.
Love has become much harder to picture lately.
There seems no time exists when her
feathers are not getting ruffled, or
when I don't have to try harder
and harder just to keep her happy.

Sometime I hope that she will
settle down and relax, perhaps begin
to meticulously preen and coo.
Then the fun part of living might
begin again in earnest.
If I ever had a clue how to do that,

it is gone now.
I placed my bird's nest in a cage.
Free range Love left to peck out a living
somewhere else where I can't hope
to interfere with the outcomes.

Lessons in Pride

Lately real life and death events played out
too close at hand.
Norman had recurring bouts of severe indigestion.
His vehement denials resulted in a sudden, fatal heart attack.
The happy goodbye I had so recently said suddenly
became a deeply disturbing memory.
An ironic finality set in and his death rattled me.
Needless worries hijacked my thoughts.
I began fretting over one imagined disaster
after another befalling everyone I knew or cared about.
Endless piles of procrastinations accumulated
in my everyday life while I daydreamed of disasters.

His pride broke my fall.
It was not derived from self-conceit, his various
lucrative decisions or his aggrandizements.
Norman's pride cost him his life.
It has become my best defense against
what happens when life lets me fall down hard,
thinking that I might never rise again.
When things go horribly wrong
I no longer get to jump to conclusions
in order to get past my sudden,
overbearing difficulties.
I can feel the pain of powerlessness, but I can't
do a damned thing about it.
Norman's pride makes me wait and take deep breaths
while things get sorted out in their own time.
I can no longer afford to ignore all the possible
consequences which, for so long,
I chose to simply grit and bear.

I continue to pensively await outcomes
while I am marooned with my powerlessness.
This lesson is rewriting itself daily.
Sometimes the script changes are hard to keep up with.
I am getting the hang of change.
At last a head weary, humbled Superman can retreat
to his inner sanctum, draw the blinds and weep.

The Raptor's Roost

I loathe to be vanquished by my shortcomings
especially when my eminent defeat is realized.
Capitulations are heartlessly demanded.
Instead, I reluctantly attempt to postpone my submission
until the anguish of inaction has become unbearable.
For a moment my eyes close and I imagine my plight
in a different, more palatable way.

Perched high on a ledge is a raptor's roost.
It is a large nest with plenty of room for me.
The drop into nothingness from there seems
both alluring and foreboding.
Fear assaults sensibility as I ponder the plunge.
No human can wrest solace from the grip of certain
terror which stares back stark and cold
from such heights.
Fear threatens like the jagged edged teeth
of a broken window glass through which
I am forced to escape.

Staring downward I see that my feet
have been replaced with talons.
My shoulders have sprouted feathers,
black and glistening, beautifully tufted
in white and grey.
My avian eyes can see for miles
and centuries further than now.

In another moment, in another shape I am
renewed and pleasantly calm.
The rough cliff face holds no attraction for me.

Gravity is no longer a conquering force
with which I must actively reckon.
Excited giddiness raises hackles
on my freshly feathered form as freedom
courses through my veins once more.
One terrible leap and the wind jerks me upward.
I rise like a birthday kite resisting a taut string.
An invisible binding anchor holds me steady.
The distant cloud shapes beckon.
A wide expanse of sky seems reserved
for my leisurely wandering as I soar high above
the deep canyons which crawl beneath me.
I am enthralled by the ever marching foothills below
as they parade by in uninterrupted ranks.
Steady currents of pleasant sensations
support me, buoy my fragile framework.
Warm risers aid an illustrious ascent.
Propelled above the receding valley floor
I effortlessly traverse vast distances
beyond today toward unseen tomorrows.
My worries float away like the wispy clouds
painted on the spotless summer skies.

Grief and Her Three Sisters

Grief is a keening widow who sits in
her room with a broad view of her lovely
courtyard just outside bay windows.
She weeps despondently and tries to calm herself.
Veiled and dressed in black,
her three sisters stand dutifully mourning
by her side.

First and most steadfast is Memory,
who holds Grief's hand and wipes her
cheek once in a while with her handkerchief
made of forgotten regrets.

Grief's youngest sister, Vain Hope,
softly whispers consolations into
Grief's inattentive ears.
This is not the end. Do not believe
what happened here was real, she murmurs.
Vain Hope tightly holds the drawstrings
to the blackout curtains of the present,
ready to block any bright ray of sunlight that
might attempt to shine in.

With a stiff, straight back and a
purposeful gait, Grief's middle sister,
False Pride, paces back and forth muttering,
This was all avoidable.
It should never have happened to
good people like us.
She pauses her pacing to pat Grief's other hand.

If it were my decision I would have
done things much differently.

Poor Grief, grateful for all the attention,
shudders and tries again to cope.
If I were just a bit stronger I would not let this
unfortunate set of circumstances upset me.
She stares outside at the courtyard where a group
of small sparrows has been foraging for crumbs.
They seems so happy flitting around under the benches,
not at all concerned that they may starve
today if they do not find sustenance.

Grief wipes her tear stained face with
her sleeve and tries to smile.
Thank you, my kind sisters for keeping me
company, but I wish to be alone right now.
Please leave me while I compose myself.

As the last sister files out of the room
Grief notices that one of the little sparrows
has found a scrap of toast that fell
to the ground during yesterday's breakfast.
She muses to herself, How lucky that little bird is to have
found the courage to keep searching for what she needed.

With some difficulty she rises from her chair and
goes outside to sit in the sun
while she contemplates her own happiness.

My Forever Pending Success

At thirteen I earned my own money.
Working a paying job meant that I didn't
have to listen to anyone else.
No one could control me as long as
I took care of my own bills.
Ever since then I have used this need to be
financially self-sufficient
as both a crutch and a mask to help me
remain excruciatingly independent.
These have also been my excuses to avoid
my family, my friends and other individuals who
might have taught me some of the skills
I desperately needed to be popular and successful.

I wanted to go it alone.
I wanted to be a prima donna,
a struggling Bohemian underdog,
flawed, charming and lucky.
I wanted to be the type of man
everyone secretly hopes
will be successful someday.

I still enjoy that self-sufficiency role
too much to give it up.
I never feel like I have attained my goals
or achieved my best at anything.
Instead, I play a game with myself in which
I constantly fight tremendous odds,
run behind schedule and try to catch up
with where I think I should be.

I never completely attain my aspirations, either.
It's small wonder that I feel unsuccessful
even when what I do seems stupendous
in the eyes of others.
Instead of basking in my successes
I almost always end up disappointed,
never feeling like I have impressed myself very much.
While I have often placed laurels on the heads of others,
at the same time I heaped ashes on my own.

A great writer once told me that if I was ever
completely satisfied with my poems
I was probably not a very good poet.
Having read and internalized this comment it seems
to me that I might finally be on the right track.

Walking in the Moonlight

Bare feet lightly tread the dusty trail beneath them.
Midnight moon has bathed the steeps in sudden brightness.
Heavy cloaked the shadowed specters hide in darkness.
Restless moon feet slowly saunter up the high tracks.
Saucer eyes scan darkened paths for crawling dangers.

Saddened half-moon fondly strokes the dusky branches.
Silver beams embellish all they lightly tincture.
Darkened trails play tag with sparsely scattered boulders.
Smiling half-moon beams its nuanced glow of grandeur.

Greedily the hungry moon surveys the shadows,
seemly sights to drink in with the cooling darkness.
Careless specters are devoured with a flourish.
Some escape along the rocky tracks undaunted.
Hoggish half-disc gorges from its silver goblet
as it scales the jagged spine of the red canyon.

From his weary skull bright orbs peer into darkness.
Over filled with hasty thoughts he tires of thinking.
Roaming mind pursues another welcome feeling.
Here he never really feels like he is lonely.
Plans intrude distractions to divert his roaming.

Lingered doubts that what's ahead will satisfy him.
Many years have passed since he has really felt this.
He peers deeply at the dim lit winding pathway.
Rock strewn summit is the goal he's almost mastered.
Rugged promontory high above the desert;
perfect place to lay his burdens down and linger.

Restless world makes plans he cannot hope to fathom.
Night sounds calm his shattered nerves into relaxing.
Croaking solemn moon prayers come to soothe his fretting.
In the bosom of the night he will rest lightly.

Wolves' howls raise the goose bumps on his weary shoulders.
Thick sliced layers made of silence quickly peel off.
Barred from shouting they are tossed into the canyon.
Peaceful mood he sorely hoped for is soon threatened.
Rustles in the pinon pines stir up a warning.
Gusty sighs lavished by listless dappled heavens.

Baked stones staid his suborn feet from their slow progress.
Savored smells collude to wake his dormant taste buds.
Creosote and sage brush blossoms tinge his nostrils.
Night air wafts its lasting leisure scents he longed for.

Flights of fancy threaten him with ruined roaming.
Half-moon whispers throaty promises to hold him.
Half-dreams lure him with visions to believe in.
Set above a darkened canyon on a hilltop
peace waits for him to come walking 'round the corner.
Moonlight walking is the medicine for many
who find nothing else can give them their elation
or produce the welcomed changes that they live for.

A Tiny Grain of Sugar

A tiny grain of sugar
rolls 'round between my fingers.
Reminds me just how very small
in the scheme of things I am.

The day outside is dawning,
a thunderstorm is stalling.
The clouds vibrate high heavens like
angels bowling in the air.

Sky rivers rage in torrents,
wild waterfalls above us.
Dust settled by the drenching rains
turns my driveway into mud.

I see a sickly glowing,
no sun to gently warm me.
No solace to replace the gloom
that my losing you has caused.

Another day will pass me,
I'll think of you and wonder
how dear your life has been to me,
why you had to leave so soon.

Onward my mind will ramble
to find I've gotten nowhere,
save for the murky confines
of the place between my ears.

If I Could Buy a Rainbow

If I could buy a rainbow
to place in your cold heart
to let its love light start
to help someone like you
and break the bond of hate.
I swear it's not too late.
If I could buy a rainbow
to place in your cold heart.

If I could find the courage
to reach my hand to you
to show that we are two.
Who knows what might begin.
We might create a pact
that puts the world on track.
If I could find the courage
to reach my hand to you.

Barely Awakening

Time's soft laid sands have filled my sleeping eyes.
Their dried out, crinkled lids struggle to rise.
My troubles napped, now rush to fill my mind.
The crack of dawn arrives to wake the blind.

Outside this cavern of a skull so void
events unspooled are recklessly deployed.
My drowsy mind is shaken with alarm,
then silenced, the foul warning tome disarmed.

The cloak of darkness torn by shafts so bright,
hangs tattered, harshly shredded by the light.
The callous day rejoices at my ire.
A few more minutes I hoped to retire.

Now buried rest my castles made of sand
by Today, a fresh shovel in its hand.

The Heavy Hand of Destiny

The heavy hand of Destiny unmercifully falls
on those born out of hopeful circumstances.
A heaving mass of vacuous foreboding
pervades their humble lives, eating holes
in their clothes like hungry moths
turned loose in the woolen's closet.

These words were never meant to be spoken aloud.
Mere mumbled uncertainties hidden away
in statistics full of cold numbers.
Sometimes they went untold altogether
or came forth faintly whispered
in guarded fashion by those who witnessed
bodies being kicked into the ditches.
Little children snickered and pointed
with immaculately clean fingers
at their shabby rags and muddy brogans.
Shame was their only birthday present.

Circumstance and accidents of birth
have rewarded their efforts to rise
with swift punches to their stomachs.
They pessimistically wait for Fairy Godmothers
to bring them the lives they were promised.
Lives they were told they did not deserve.
Hope writhes and struggles to rise to its knees.
Hope is weaker and fails them again and again.

Freedom is a relentless idealist.
Freedom roams wherever its surer substance will allow
it space and belly laughs in echoing guffaws,

which sound both pitifully near and far away.
Freedom voices aloud those simpler truths
which will one day come home to roost.
Freedom waits like a pillowed dream upon which
the hopeless may someday rest their tormented heads.
Freedom bellows its dream to any who might listen.
An outlandish, unheard of dream that all current
travails will disappear like the mists
after dawn breaks, frighteningly bright and hard to watch.
Stubborn sorrows will ease and disturbed
memories will cause them to cringe no more.
They will waste no more time reliving hard knocks endured.
There will be nothing left to hold them back or
keep them locked out of the Promised Land.

Lives of poverty come barren of contentment.
Poverty is disdained for its poverty.
No longer will circumstance force poor people
to indulge their economic betters,
to give in to the tyrannies of social oppression.

There will be no bleak, for-ordained, presumptive
claims on their lands, their bodies or their dreams:
claims designed to vex these unfortunate souls
living on the boundaries of our Great Social Order.
Un-denied, their triumphs will flock and flourish,
no longer watching and waiting for better times
to come before they proudly fly about cawing victory.

Faired resources and respect will be their ticket
to finally ride at the front of the bus.
They will live with courageous intentions,

taste the sweet pleasure of accomplishment,
unpretentiously flaunt glories gained,
victories sorely won to accolades galore.

No price is too great to pay,
no feat too perilous for a people who,
collectively, have nothing more to lose.
Freedom felt is not freedom won.
Freedom won is forever felt and
revered by all posterity.

For What I'm Worth

Relentless conscience driven by my fears
has shouted loudly in my deafened ears,
reminding me that deeds now need to mend.
No longer may I scoff and then pretend
that this is different, not for me to feel.
Where I have erred the consequence was real.

In actions and in thoughts I was disgraced.
My manifold, low motives were misplaced.
The worth of man is in his deeds achieved,
not in his hopes, imagined or believed.
I am responsible today and true:
my actions, not intentions, are my due.

My truth is mine, no other to set blame,
just as alone into this world I came.
No one waits here to set me on the course.
Alone I ride, with reins I steer this horse
of truth that takes me through the life ahead,
till at the end I lay me down for dead.

Move Your Mountain

Take up the pickaxe and strike at your roots.
Keen knowledge may yet grace your sweaty brow
when rippling muscle has failed you.
The sledge hammer sweetly whispers,
Grasp me by the neck and swing.

Endless hollow thoughts need smashing up.
While you still know how,
harmlessly dismantle the lies.
Your sacredly guarded beliefs
have grieved you long enough.

Wrought iron excuses glow white
in truth's forge.
Sloughed ash and cinders tell
their awful, twisted renditions.
They spill their dross and fracture
all life's carefully formed molds again.

Pitiful sums of nothingness bubble and churn.
Amalgams of untruths form distorted castings.
Meaningless, molten puddles of futility writhe
trapped within your smoking, hollow mouth.
Quickly poured and left to cool too fast,
they have warped and cracked,
become useless to all in the end.

Sibilant shrieks vibrate your guilty mind
as the pickaxe clearly, calmly
enunciates its ever present message:
Dig like your life depends on it.

Dig till you find yourself
then, dig deeper and discover
who you really are.

Acknowledgments

Thank you to all my friends and fellow poets who encourage me all the time to write more poetry. To Tommy Welch for putting music to my poems and Rainy Kimbrough for singing them and giving me space on their stage gigs to read from my last book. My heartfelt thanks to fellow authors Myrtle Thomas, Hiram Larew and Joyce Kessel for their help and encouragement, as well.

Special thanks to Nick Courtright, Kyle McCord, Cameron Finch, Alex Kale, Erin Larson, Ronaldo Alves, Kevin Stone, and all of the team at Atmosphere Press for helping me edit and refine my ideas, and for taking a chance on an unknown poet. Thank you to my readers for your generous reviews and support. Your kindness and helpful comments do not go unappreciated.

Credits

In order of their appearance in this book the following poems were previously published online on the poetry site, allpoetry.com.

About
Atmosphere Press

Atmosphere Press is an independent, full-service publisher for excellent books in all genres and for all audiences. Learn more about what we do at atmospherepress.com.

We encourage you to check out some of Atmosphere's latest releases, which are available at Amazon.com and via order from your local bookstore:

Gnostic Triptych, poetry by Elder Gideon

For the Moment, poetry by Charnjit Gill

Battle Cry, poetry by Jennifer Sara Widelitz

I woke up to words today, poetry by Daniella Deutsch

Never Enough, poetry by William Guest

Second Adolescence, poetry by Joe Rolnicki

Z is for Zapatazo, poetry by Ruben Rivera

Until *the Kingdom Comes*, poetry by Jeanne Lutz

Warcrimes, poetry by GOODW.Y.N

The Freedom of Lavenders, poetry by August Reynolds

Convalesce, poetry by Enne Zale

Poems for the Bee Charmer (And Other Familiar Ghosts), poetry by Jordan Lentz

Serial Love: When Happily Ever After... Isn't, poetry by Kathy Kay

Flowers That Die, poetry by Gideon Halpin

Through The Soul Into Life, poetry by Shoushan B

Embrace The Passion In A Lover's Dream, poetry by Paul Turay

Drifters, poetry by Stuart Silverman

About
the Author

Jerry Lovelady is the author of an earlier book of poetry published by Atmosphere Press in 2021 titled *Other Worlds, in Other Words*. Lovelady is married to his muse of 26 years, Kristi, and lives in Beaumont, Texas. He divides his time between writing poetry, doing chores around the house and substitute teaching.

He enjoys traveling, which provides him with many inspirations for his poetry. His subjects are taken from real life events, from his past experiences and some are projections of his inner workings which many authors cringe to reveal. Lovelady writes with a remarkable subtlety that permeates most of his more personal poems. His writings demonstrate his passion for individual freedoms and rejection of the oppressive limitations modern society places on individuals to conform.

Lovelady's poetry reflects an insightful, almost mystic approach to poetic expression. His style often intentionally leaves the reader with a feeling of edginess or uncertainty. His poems tend to pry apart the wrappings of his internal emotional conflicts, as other poetry does, displaying what he finds there in a more spiritual context that directs the reader toward redemption of the human spirit more than toward a stark, surreal escapism.

Lovelady writes about the natural and supernatural forces he believes are at work behind the scenes, bending our wills, naturally driving us to search for our answers in the clues which life seems to aimlessly scatter about.

A prolific poet, Lovelady is currently working on his next book which should be completed sometime near the end of 2023.

Comments and reviews of Jerry Lovelady's books are encouraged and may be directed to the author's website, **jerryloveladypoetry.com**.

BUY

Other Worlds, in Other Words

Also from Atmosphere Press,
more poems by Jerry Lovelady:

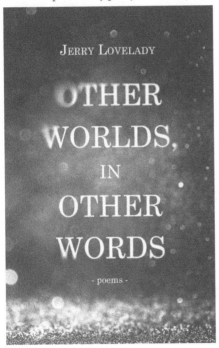

See more about
this book here:

CPSIA information can be obtained
at www.ICGtesting.com
Printed in the USA
BVHW042205151122
652066BV00003B/44